LOGIC AND TH

Love poems 1999-2003

AF Harrold

Two Rivers Press

First published in the UK in 2004 by
Two Rivers Press
35-39 London Street
Reading
RG1 4PS

A CIP catalogue record for this book is available
from the British Library.

ISBN 1901 677 38 9

The publisher acknowledges financial assistance
from the Arts Council of England.

Printed and bound in England by Conservatree
Print & Design Ltd, Caversham, Reading.

CONTENTS

Bear Song

When I'm alone I take off my skin
and expose the hair
      and muscle within.

I stand upright breathing slow
at the door of my cave,
      growling low.

Often the days are long
and I marvel at the world's working
      though everything is wrong.

Misanthropic as rock or stone
I scowl at the sunset.
      I live alone.

SECTION I

Nine Pieces

I. *Poem*

As a child I was always the strange boy who locked himself
in his bedroom of an evening secretly reading the dictionary.
Its world, you see, was bounded but immense; roomy enough to get lost in
and yet those uncrossable cloth-bound borders were profoundly comforting.

And so today it is with little surprise I find the dictionary open in my lap
so soon after we have finished speaking on the phone about my father.
Without thinking, I am idly flicking through from page to page, a little dazed.

I didn't plan to end up here but here we are, and trailing my finger along I read,
after **4. embolism**, a further entry. A stroke, it says, is simply another word
for a **solidus**, especially when one is reading aloud.

I follow back a few pages and discover that the solidus was once a golden
    Byzantine coin,
and that in later years this coin's name became applied to the Mediaeval shilling
and found itself being written down as a long *s*, which, in time, became the
    mark we use
to divide information into portions and to show the alternatives or fractions
    of a thing.

II. Being There

While I wasn't looking my father grew up,
and then he grew old, and then he grew down.

And now he's becoming smaller and smaller,
as if his clothes manage to remain life size
while he falls away, deeper into the distance.

And time is falling away from him too, it seems,
so sometimes he forgets to be here and now,
gliding back towards infancy, the grown man gone.

And I remember an ancient picture of myself,
a small child photographed in the garden,
dressed in only a t-shirt and *his* milkman's hat.

And I am aware of how little separates us, now and then,
as he stands quiet in the front room, in just his vest,
suddenly unable to recall any motive for his being there.

III. Song (Unfinished)

There's a skeleton in my father's bed
and the skeleton looks like him.

I'll walk round the block one more time,
one more time before I go in.

He's in the room that my brother had,
that he had until he left home;

he's in the room that then was mine
until I had also gone.

Now there's a skeleton in my father's bed
and the skeleton looks like him.

I'll walk round the block one more time,
one more time before I go in.

He's laid in the bed that we all have shared,
that we've dreamt in one by one,

he's

IV. Qualities I Had

Today I am grown weak.
Weak like a snake, say:
unable to lift you;
unable to look you in the eye,
I am grown too low.

Yesterday I had some strength.
Yesterday I caught that train,
made that long journey.
I arrived in the dark of the night,
I pushed my way through the dark,
fought my way through the dark,
brushed aside the dark and made my way to you.

But arriving beside you this morning
everything seemed to fail.
What qualities I had,
what qualities I thought I had,
what qualities I hoped to have,
all slipped away.
I heard the final drip as the gutters did their jobs.
The splash of liquid qualities into liquid everything.
A long way down.

Today I am grown so weak,
so weak that I am almost afraid to say it,
but I'm afraid it has to be said.

Your hands have grown cold.
Your body has become bony.
Your bones have grown fragile.
I know your eyes are not going to open again.
Your breaths rasp on their way out
and scrape on their way in.

I am grown as weak as you today,
on my knees I am shaped like that serpent,
finding it hard to be entirely human,
humanity seeming to have no place in this room.

V. Four Rhythms

It's the night before the day of my father's funeral
and I'm laid out in a bath in the house I once lived in.

It's dark. It's been dark since I switched off the light
and I switched off the light to switch off the fan
which at this time of night's louder than anything.

And after a minute it spins to a stop
and just for a moment the room is in silence.

But just as grey sight replaces the darkness
so noises emerge from silence's corners.
And as the night passes I notice four rhythms.

The first and the fastest and faintest is fire,
like a wood burning fire there's this crackle as bubbles
constantly fall into nothing but water,

it's a background static like the infra-red glow
that the Hubble has seen behind everything.

Then the slowest of rhythms, the clear drip of the cistern,
so slow I can't tell if it's random or fixed,
I lose count or count faster or think that I might've,

and just as I'm sure that it's stopped then it drips,
just once. Then I wait and I wait and my focus

shifts with the waiting and I'm caught by the clock
that I hadn't even known was kept in the bathroom.

It's probably pocket sized, a bedside sized thing,
sat on the window-sill next to the mirror
that hasn't been shaved in for several weeks.

I'm assuming it has a second long period,
but with no independent method of checking
I'm simply assuming, but it seems about right.

It's quiet, but like a steadying hand
is a comfort tonight, as over the top

leaks the last and the loudest; so loud I'm surprised
no one's kept awake, well no one but me,
and no one is shouting or banging on walls.

Just behind and below my ears pumps my blood,
a stereo thumping at the back of my skull;

maybe the rim of the bath resonates,
amplifies what I hear, makes me aware
of the juice through my body, the animal thrust
of the pulse through my flesh.

In the darkness I count, or at least try to count,
understand what it is that I have or I am,

and at first it appears that, timed by the clock,
blood's reaching my brain twice every second,

but it soon becomes clear that it's not quite that simple
that a fall out of synch and then back into synch

occurs each three or four ticks, which I think suggests
eighty or ninety heartbeats a minute

and I lie for a moment and wonder whether
it's too fast or too slow, or just about right
but I've not done the research and so I don't know.

But I'm curious. not worried and I stare in the dark
at the greyed cabinets and, through the mirror, the window
where a streetlight shines pale, dimmed by the blind

and as all of the rhythms come together one time
I think how this blood that starts in my heart
is reaching my brain, without fail, without effort,

time and again, heart to brain, heart to brain,
all the time, without thinking, heart to brain, and again.

VI. The Drawer

And this is my father's drawer
and these are his short stubby pens
brought home from the bookie's
and these are his pencils
blunt at the point and capped
with gritty blue or red rubbers
and these are his scraps of paper
all sorts of bits of paper
from places and stubs and notes
and here is his paperclip
and here is his drawing pin
and here is his elastic band
and another and another one
and here is his soft
black leather key holder
with small metal loops
attaching the keys
and here is the change
the rummage of coins
at the foot of the drawer
scattered about and amongst
all the rest of the stuff of his life
and here are the coins
that I'd help myself to
as a young growing man
when the rooms were dark
and I had to go out
and I needed a quid
and so helping myself
I would go without thinking.

VII. Ghost

In this dream I saw the things the years should keep,
as, in the kitchen, you stood as in life,
hands open to me as if I were your wife,
a scab of blood dried brown above your nose,

where you'd been bashed, no friend to gravity,
by face-first falling weakly to the ground,
as you often did when people weren't around.
But in these after days, when your ghost rose,

you weren't as thin as death's cold-calling made you.
Your eyes were dazed, shone blue in your confusion,
as if I looked to you like the illusion.
The words you spoke were thin things, and afraid.

You touched me then. A farewell form we chose
by embracing in the kitchen of a home
we'd both left, in our ways, some time ago;
me to live and you to cease to be.

It was a night when dreaming came too close
and cast its shadow across the following day,
and into evening that shadow fought to stay.
I vainly hoped to block it out with sleep.

VIII. Living

'Take care.' Those were the last words that my father said to me.
Small words, common ones that were unthinkingly said,
but which resonate now each time they're said by someone else;
unnoticed pleasantries, easy words that slip out unprepared.

I'd never noticed how often this advice got passed around,
from one to another and to another human being–
how fragile and forgetful we're supposed to be, needing
to be reminded at each turn that it's a tricky thing, living.

Perhaps he'd said it to me before, but if he did I did forget.
I see him say it now, tired, sat up and shrinking in that bed;
the bedroom window was south facing and it was August then,
the picture's clear, and the next time that I saw him he was dead

or nearly dead. And people still remind me to 'Take care,'
as if, somehow, by caring enough such things might change,
but more likely, I suspect, is that by always being careful
or by never being so, things, that is the world, will stay the same.

Apologia

Time is stretching out now, stretching finely,
so fine I'm almost afraid it's going to snap,
crack and fly away from me, or else snap back,
leave a red welt slapped across my face.

It is all the important things that have escaped,
that have faded or slipped away, or that are,
to be more correct, escaping, fading, slipping;
they are with me still, but barely within reach.

The unimportant things don't remain either,
but it doesn't matter that they're gone, or going.
Unimportant things are like that: pale gems perhaps,
or like handsome coins whose currency is lost.

I look at everything. Everything is laid before me,
like a country, blue in the night's thin light,
and I barely find the landmarks, trace you out.
Tonight I think I see your face in a knotted hillside.

Section II

Of all forms of caution, caution in love
is perhaps the most fatal to true happiness.

Bertrand Russell, *Marriage & Morals,* 1929.

How To Avoid Bears

I have read many times and in many different sources
that the best way to not be eaten by bears
is to lie still and silent on the ground before them.

This is good advice, if it works, but better is, surely,
to not be attractive to bears. Do not smell like honey.
Do not move like a fish. Do not breathe like you like bears.

On Love

And just inside this heart I see a certainty raising its head,
giving the lie, utterly, to my famed belief in not knowing.

And now I can feel the warmth of the air on my arms
and the trail of a comet caught in an ellipse around the sun
shines dimly in the dark sky as it passes the orbit of Venus.

I step indoors, closing the door, shutting out further portents,
leaving the future to its own devices for a short while,
while I run a bath and find my place in this or that book.

And thinking absently in one direction or another it seems clear
that this heart is certain and I grow troubled by its certainty.

In another room I hear the kettle finish boiling. But I sit still,
feeling that amid the steam there is certainty. Amid the peace too.
Wherever I go it seems to come along with me and I blink,
worrying constantly that this dumb heart has grown so sure.

Poem (380)

Everything gets struck by lightning now and again,
and to believe that you could be any different
is a basic error in judgement.

You are not immune to these monumental
and indiscreet occurrences anymore than
the Earth can help orbiting or the sky can help falling.

Instead, remember that from time to time
and in the most obscure ways patterns are forming
and that however hard you try to remain distinct
distinctions will, eventually, always blur.

There is no preparation possible
and there has never been any use
in crying over the inevitable.

Tea Party

Love. Alice is in love.
She pours tea. Drinks tea.
Laughs. Alice is laughing.
Everyone stares at her tresses,
falling across her shoulders
and down the back of her dress.
Alice impresses. She pours tea.
Everyone drinks. She's in love.
The feeling is settling in her stomach,
like a morsel of cake, eaten once.
Now it is at rest, the world pauses.
As the light slows to zero, colours dim.
This only takes a second. Or less.
Everyone's talking, madly.
She looks around. She wonders.
'Has anyone noticed the change?'
But they fuss to themselves,
seemingly unaltered by the absolute
altering experience of love. Love.
Alice is in love. She is sure,
in her stomach, just beside her heart,
something has settled, has been settled.
She looks around at the party.
She sips her tea. Longs under her breath.
Imagines scribbling a name on her jotter
beside some distant river. Long ago.
And now she knows. Alice is in love.

Small Vows

I want to read Ludwig Wittgenstein to you,
bring water that's now wine to you,
reverse time for you.

I'd like to, though I know I never will, for you,
pick up every bill for you,
be still for you.

Understand, and like, all that's not quite right with you,
only infrequently fight with you,
catamite for you.

And In The Moment In-Between Letters

And in the moment in-between letters and phone calls and e-mails
and kisses and sightlines and trembling hands,
and in the moment between holding and sleeping and eating
and breathing and waking and walking and and and...
there is a silence, there is a spinning sense of balance
as everything revolves without and the falling dust illuminates.

This is the moment when all realisation concentrates,
when the places slot around the pieces and the heart is light.

This is the moment when, wherever you are, it's ok,
when the awareness grows of exactly which word it was you'd been
    looking for.

And then the phone begins to ring and it's her voice from the distance
or the postman lets slip an envelope addressed with her handwriting
and it begins again and you are involved and the heart is light.

Two Lines

This is the night when things come together,
when all ports are possible in any kind of weather.

Three Lines In The Morning

And in the morning your nightshirt grows too thin
and light and warmth and your body begin to sing
and being no saint, I must say, I give in.

Room Poem, #2

And in the first moment of the morning a ritual begins
the blanket draws back slightly, with a draught, and you slip in
asking a single question as you slide close – 'Did you dream?'

And still sleeping or waking or somewhere just between
eyes and mouth co-ordinate, barely, with the messages within
and a voice is found to intimate just where it is I've been.

With these walls, these windows, doors and space there's room
    enough to dream
and though a certain amount of meaning's lost there's still something
    there that seems
to be some sort of truth or revelation or something else that gleams.

*

At some point slightly later, more awake, I leave this room
and the rain falls on the pavement and my thinking turns to you
and then work begins or something else and old patterns just resume
and whatever insight woke with me is now sinking out of view
and everything I know now is, it seems, just what I always knew.

Private Language Argument

Don't turn on the tv.
There's nothing there. There never was.
Whatever was before was never something much.

No. Switch the wireless to silence.
Leave the record player unplugged.
Forget the music that fills the days with its insistencies.

Come close this afternoon. Put down the books.
Do not concern yourself with the bookmark.
There is little difference from page to page.

Draw the curtains over the windows.
Turn the paintings to the wall.
Hold out instead for the message of this body.

Do not expect the telephone to ring.
Listen only to the movements of this mouth.
Ignore the poems, they are true only half the time.

Room Poem, #1a

This room has grown deeper, has grown larger.
In the presence of awe it has become somewhere more holy.
It has become somewhere where rest is possible.

Through my hands and through my breath the walls have moved back,
the ceiling has lifted. The doorway has located itself.
Now there is no need for anyone to wander lost, here.

Everywhere I look I see wonder. The window is shuttered
but the room, the landscape is bright enough for any activity.
I ask only one question here – here amongst all this peace

and amongst all this time and space and light and love,
how will it ever be possible for me to sleep at night?

Room Poem, #1b

This room has grown deeper, has grown larger.
There are warm spots in the sunlight, in the silence,
where civilisations meet and where letters arrive.

This room is open to itself, communicates with itself
without listening to angels or demons or men or women.
There are paths in this room I have not discovered.

This room has grown from my hands and from my words.
It has taken to itself poetry and has made it lighter,
more meaningful, more beautiful, has made itself song.

This room is open to the heavens, holds out its arms to the stars.
There are nebulae, in this room, that glow faintly but distinctly in the air,
pausing in revolution, in birth, before passing away.

This room has grown into something both unexpected
and expected, has become light and nature and rapture.
There is furniture among the valleys and windowsills.

*

I sit on the bed, in this room, staring nakedly into the distance,
listening to the sound of a shoreline, listening to the night,
listening eventually to the space that has become my room.

Nature Poem

Be still. I am the Bear from your dreams.
I walk with the forests and I walk at night.
I am broader than grasslands.
I am broader than auroras and leaves.
I am elsewhere.
I am the Bear from your dreams.

I hold the day in my claw and move about it.
I prowl cliff-tops and valleys.
I span oceans.
At night I am still warm,
even in the dark, even in the winter.
I smell of safety and of solitude and of longing.

When I am away it is because I am hungry.
It is because I am walking, looking,
perhaps it is because I am searching for something.
I do not always know.
My heart beats like a whale's, crossing continents.
Some days I am blue like the stars.

I am the Bear from your dreams.
I walk with the forests and I sleep in your arms.
And I sleep long. And I sleep deep.
Be still. I am the Bear from your dreams.

Exuberant Biographical Fragment

It is summer and you still wear your winter coat.
Perhaps it is time for a change of residence.
Let us move to Florence, where those poets lived.
Where the climate is conducive to... well... love.

Let us become wanderers on the map.
Let us write our lives on the wind, on mountainsides.

Today we must eat,
but tomorrow we'll begin our vagrancy of art,
our daytrip through immortality.
Let us leave just enough meat for the biographers.
The rest we can leave on the wind, like music.

Subtle Animals

Hand on hand on hand on hand
they lie together and together, he and her.

The windows are open and the air moves
and rolls and flows across sweat and backs

and hand on hand and hand on hand,
and together they cry, their tears happy

and drying even as they emerge, laughing,
onto their cheeks. Those were the days.

And Looking Back

Sometimes a hand in or of or from the past can make us come
alive again without our realising what it is that's being done.

And sometimes bodies find their ways from where they each began,
a surprise curving into the present, into the light, under the hand,
and without warning or comment everything on hold has suddenly begun
and now, it seems, this is not as bad as it could possibly have become
and for a while there's only time and flesh to pass before the rising sun.

And it happens that tonight is a night picked from a hundred and one
other possible nights, each spinning lost between the stars in the silence from
the closing mouths of kisses and answers and the lover's tongue
to the morning that in the end is well known to always come.

And looking back, what is there that has not yet been remarked upon,
the resistance of memory to education of any form,
or the ritual days of living that nights like this can pluck us from?

.

A Short Story

She listened to Petrushka and was constantly surprised.
They laughed about it later as he lay between her thighs–
'That's what Stravinksy does to me,' he confidently lied.

Poem (538)

Before he opens the door to bid her goodnight
he looks for a moment into her face
and can't be sure but thinks he sees some trace
of love there, although it's awkward in this light.

And after embracing goodbye he shuts the door
and leans against it for a moment, breathing.
He hadn't counted on this feeling at her leaving,
as if that farewell held a hint of something more

substantial held off in the future, but not far.
And with this warming thought he goes to bed,
imprinted with her scent in heart and head.
And lying awake he hears the alarm of some car

alone in the night, and remembers being a child
as headlights crossed the ceiling, and how she smiled.

On Stars

One night when we were walking late on our way home,
not quite hand in hand but somewhere close,
looking up at the high dark sky overhead
you pointed Sirius out to me and said
how someone had once shown it there to you.

And we wondered then about the stars,
how at such distance they all look much the same,
some brighter, some dimmer, some burning coldly with a bluer flame,
but how few, at the final count, we could ever know by name.

And looking down then, from the sky to you,
I saw both street- and moonlight flash across your eyes
and watched the glister of those two lights shift
as you softly turned your head from me to speak
to those countless stars unknown and out of reach.

Dream Poem, #1

In the last dream before waking they kissed
and took hold of each opportunity so narrowly and so wholly missed,
took hold of that which, for one reason or another, had never quite
    managed to exist,
in the last dream before waking, once, they kissed

and in kissing they made a small vow of this—
to hold onto one another by mouth or waist or wrist,
to hold on, now that they'd been found, to hold and not relinquish
and in kissing they made a small vow of this

but small vows, it appears, are not enough,
for with morning dreams become things distant and seen only in parts,
    from above,
and each, waking apart, realised that dreaming is something less than love
and, finally, it seems, small vows are never quite enough

but through days they carried with them the warming knowledge of this—
that in the last dream before waking, once, they kissed.

And One Day You Notice

And one day you notice that there is no further work to be done,
that everything you had planned or expected to do is over, is gone,
or else no longer seems quite as important as it did when first begun.

And this evening the evening is bright and the sunlight is still warm
and somewhere on the desk is unimportant paperwork, some form
or other that once seemed the only way left to hold back the storm
that threatened itself as the inevitable result of that single straw you'd drawn.

But now it seems there is nothing important enough to call out to you or touch
you deep enough to distract you from what you used to love so much,
which was to think that there'd be time enough before you turned to dust.

And tonight, although the telephone rings out against the window frame,
there is no need, no urgency to answer it, for it's certain it will ring again
and through the glass you see clouds that shift and pass before the flame
of individual stars which, it is likely, have simply a number and no name.

Watching The Sunset Silhouetting Trees

Watching the sunset silhouetting trees
I am reminded of nothing.

It is a beautiful feeling, freedom.

Some Quiet Morning

On some quiet morning when he hasn't gone to work
he sits in the front room and sees the sun white outside the window
and remembers something that nudges a thought of something else into view

and he ponders on how, since you've gone, the only thing he has kept of you
is a dream you once had–
about how, drifting in the night near the sea, you were sleeping

tight and small and safe in the arms of a bear
and of how the sound of the waves breaking became breathing
and the sound of breathing became waves.

And now it is nearly lunchtime and he walks into the kitchen
and opens a can of soup.
It is winter still and, at times, hibernation seems an attractive option.

The Right Shapes

What is clear is that any void that you left when you left
has now been filled. The right shapes have been moving,
have been lining themselves up through the years
and through the meetings, e-mails, phone calls, readings,
through the weeks and through the glances, words, letters,
through the days and through the hands, mouths, clothing,
through the minutes and seconds. The right shapes
have fallen, slotted, whispered into place and there is no void.

As he lifts your latest letter from the mat he recognises
the post-mark and the handwriting and opens it as he moves
further into the flat. So, you're married now. He is happy.

'It Is Nothing. Wonders Pass.'

See there, there is a light in the sky,
it is a comet or a sign.

It is a gentle light,
white smudged between the stars.

It moves from night to night.
It appears in no records.

Perhaps everything is at peace tonight
or perhaps the peace is fragile.

It is midnight-cold and dark.
The moon is new. It has grown late.

The game is waiting inside,
there is cinnamon and the fire is warm.

Something Lost

Examining what was good and free
I happened across something lost,
something left by itself, out in the woods, one day.

It was shaped like a snake in the sun,
warm and smooth and slender,
as green as me and as still as the summer.

Having no pockets to speak of and, besides,
not wishing, really, to take it home with me
I moved it a little to one side.

Curving my hands under its belly
I lifted it in one slow movement and shifted it
into the leaves at the edge of the path.

Its eyes regarded me lazily,
though not dumbly,
as I walked on further into the woods

happy with the knowledge that it would now
take more than a hapless foot
to crush so nice a serpent.

Section III

But now irrationally I was seized by a strange worship,
not, surely of the star, that mere furnace which mere
distance falsely sanctified, but of something other,
which the dire contrast of the star and us signified
to the heart. Yet what, what could thus be signified?
Intellect, peering beyond the star, discovered no Star
Maker, but only darkness; no Love, no Power even,
but only Nothing. And yet the heart praised.

Olaf Stapledon, *Star Maker,* 1937.

Putting All Talk Of Stars To One Side

Putting all talk of stars to one side,
ignoring the meaning of the heavens,
the talk of subtle currents
and the arcane mysteries of the heart,
I shall speak to you plainly, for once.

Somewhere inside the labyrinth
that is constructed from the thought of love
there is a doorway
and beyond it is a courtyard
where a fountain breaks the light into colours.

Dancing through this water,
with little regard for decorum or modesty
are naked beings, lighter than me
or you or any fleshly body,
and they are singing as they splash.

And from the wordless sounds of their song
comes a sense of contentment,
nonsensical but complete,
illiterate but understanding.
These dancers are free in ways that I am not.

Trapped in words I muddle myself
with misunderstanding and with sleight,
with ignorance and beliefs,
until, eventually, exhausted I fall
into darkness and drowsy sleep.

But somewhere in the labyrinth that contains
all variations of the human heart
there is a shaft of pure light
piercing the darkness
and there is a fountain breaking it into colours.

Song (503)

He's tired and she's tired
and there are few stars to be seen through the clouds.

Somewhere there is deep breathing
and gentle lullabies are being sung,

but he is tired and she is tired
and there are few stars in the sky tonight.

Somewhere dreaming becomes as shallow as breathing
and the dark of the silence is shifting easily

but he is tired and she is tired
and it seems stars are of less and less importance now.

Somewhere couples make love with urgency
and a television makes a living room blue

but he's tired and she's tired
and there's just one star showing at the horizon.

Poem (531)

Buying bread one morning I was reminded
 of how essential you once were to me,
of how, waking with the dawn's light
 or drifting in the dark I would reach for you,
of how, looking from sky to street
 to window to face I would note details,
store them somewhere safe in order to share
 my views of the world with you, later on.

Placing the loaf into the carrier bag
 and leaving the shop I thought how strange life is,
how sometimes it will all change around,
 how overnight omens and portents become weather
and how something as ordinary as bread
 becomes the pivot point of an ordinary morning,
as if its importance was something other than
 a brief excuse to leave your flat for a while.

And So Today Take Off My Wristwatch

It has snowed and, not venturing out, it seems we must stay in,
draw the curtains back and see the winter light reflecting in
and stay in bed or share a bath and eat straight from the tin
heedless of staining the duvet which has become a sort of skin.

And with the thermostat turned up and with the wireless switched off
we do simply simple things that we know we do not do enough
and sometimes they have something to do with lofty things like love
or passion, perhaps, or loyalty, but at other times do not.

For sometimes it must be recognised that duties have stepped in
and regulated each of the hours that we have stretched between
dawn and breakfast, work and dinner, and in time the heart wears thin,
and so today take off my wristwatch, let me lie down, breathe you in.

*

And in the silence between breathing some bird sings in the garden
and once again certain things between us start to harden.

Situations

There are a whole load of people here
and none of them understand each other.
I mean they all speak English, so really
they understand each other just fine, for what it's worth,
but underneath that they don't know what it is
that this one wants, or that one.

It may be that they don't understand themselves,
since, if they did, they'd be able to say those things out loud
and saying it out loud, finding the right words, would mean
that someone else would be able to understand it, right?
After all, that's what language is all about,
Wittgenstein and all that, right?

*

This one says he loves this other one and she,
for what it's worth, says she loves him too,
but then leaves one evening, travelling through darkness,
to arrive at some completely other destination.
And he follows, catches the wrong train, and becomes
a treasure, somehow, in someone else's life entirely.

Who understood what just happened?
What did it mean for these things to be spoken aloud
and what effect did events bear on beliefs?
If there are truths then they are subtle and hard to know,
since it is easy enough to lie, to disguise, dissemble,
I mean, after all, look at this, I am doing it right now.

On Love

It is night now. This is moonlight. That the Evening Star.
And here, the side of the tip of my index finger would move lightly
on the naked flesh that shows at the nape of your neck.

You are wearing your hair short these days.

*

Through this merest of tendernesses are communicated things,
as your lips would open to acknowledge, that would otherwise be lost,
strangled and stranded in the twin mazes of language and thought.

But I let this pass. The night is too short for philosophy.

I watch a patch of moonlight on the bedclothes.
Now the winter grows cold and tonight my little heart seems sure of itself.
All love, it says, can be contained in the keening of a single thin fingertip.

Sunday Afternoon Poem, #1

There're couples fucking in the woods on Sunday afternoons
everywhere I look and they're reminding me of you
with your knickers in a pile somewhere nowhere near your thighs
and the iridescent glister of moisture in your eyes.

Everywhere I wander on this Sunday afternoon
there are couples fucking and reminding me of you
there's a quiver in the bushes, one more whimper from the ferns,
there's just a glimpse of hairy buttock and a semi-coital gurn.

There is groaning all around me on this Sunday afternoon
and the very intonation and the phrasing's just like you
would make when we were walking, sitting, lying mouth to mouth,
when the woods were strangely empty on a Sunday afternoon,
when the birds, to grant us privacy, would choose then to migrate south
and when only Love, the bastard, would dare to kick us out.

Sometimes The Gaps Seem Greater Than The Matter

Listen,
      of course she kept a photo to remind her of the rest
and of course she promptly lost it in the movement and the peace
and now that winter's coming, and it's the only thing that is,
the cold glows through her fingertips and she can't feel any less.

*

The kitchen's feeling crowded as she turns the kettle on
but the company's merely spectral and it's the early afternoon
and as the kettle clicks to silence that's one more small job done.

The only water's cold now and the crockery's crying out
but she's caught herself thinking and she starts to turn around
but then the absence at her centre stubbornly stares her down.

*

Words spoken come to haunt her, come to call her up from sleep
where she contemplates, nightly, those things the darkness kept,
where she communicates slightly with those things that she has left.

In time she'll just turn over and she'll crawl back into sleep
but the ticking clock's a watcher, quick, dumb voyeur of the scene,
as she's crying and she's coughing and there's not much in-between.

Raft

Years have gone by, but I don't count how many.
It's late and a memory's come: a night when your dreams
and mine coincided, collided together for once.

It was a time in our lives when we'd fallen through love,
and although I don't know what I dreamt, never did,
and have even less knowledge of yours, know we found

that somewhere between them we each woke just a little,
and closed eyes, mouths and hands sought out our sexes
and things frantic and brutal occurred in the dark.

Wordless and sightless we met, clung together,
as if to a raft, lashed desperately, whipped by the rain,
and I came with a rush and sank back into sleep.

*

And then, later, the morning announced its arrival,
the column of light creeping onto the pillows,
and I woke fully up, uncertain of the waking before,

and the one thing I know, I remember for sure,
is that we neither asked what went on in the dark
or whether it might've been just our own dreaming.

But by then we were talking so little, and so little more.

Poem (598)

When I went out I had not intended to come here.
I had planned to do a few jobs, visit the Post Office,
pay in a cheque or two, and yet, here I am.

If you had a window-box I'd be able to see some life,
know how things are. But as it is all I see is the sun
glinting whitely off the glass of your windows.

Poem (381)

These are just shadows of splinters of relics
of the Saint you believed in. You loved all his grieving,
the stuttering failings, the loss and the frost
creeping over the fingers and into the mouth and the heart.
You fell at the start when you heard that he knew,
or he thought that he knew, how to do it all right,
how his song was the one, how his voice could be heard
moaning into the crowd in that place, at that time.
And that was all fine but not once did he offer
to martyr himself, as all good Saints should,
so these are just splinters and wood is just wood
and right now, you could say, at the end of the day
he just faded away.

Iscariot

There is a moment in every night,
or in every life, when the pin pricks,

when the single drop of blood falls dark,
when the realisation collapses into view

that really: there is no one else.

At this moment the darkness of a life,
or of the night, is perfected.

At this moment the only option open
is to fall down.

Whatever is seen to happen outside now,
whatever is glimpsed in the street

or the garden
can no longer be believed in or trusted.

There is a moment in every night,
and in every life, when the kiss hangs heavy

on a man's lips or cheek,
and when the only solution left is flesh.

Cosmologies

The astronomers tell us in their articles or programmes on tv
that there rotate, fat and regal, at the centre of each galaxy
black holes that are detectable because of their vast density.

And even in the Milky Way they've plotted and weighed our pivot point
and each particle that drifts through blackness into blackness joins
a thousand other particles all bound in dance descending on
this singularity which says, in time, all things to me are one.

And now, looking inwards, I feel a pull and cannot help but descend
past homunculi of lovers, colleagues, family and friends
into a heart so hard and dense I can't see if or how it ends
and now engulfed and blind and stuck I do not see the stream it sends
away across my shoulder: a glowing thread of hope that bends
out past event horizons into the macroscopic world again,
which trust and love and human warmth attempt to comprehend.

And Sometimes There Is Happiness Here

And, we discover, what happens happens not for the best but simply
    because it does.
And although the best is sometimes included in the results, sometimes
    too is dust,
and the delirium of wrong turnings in the heart, in the night, in the past
can grow heavy and sometimes the right course of action is just to say 'Enough'.

And, it is noted, when things happen they happen in their own time and
    are done
not as results of careful planning in the long afternoons under the warming sun
but on the cusp, on the wing, as an afterthought to the teetering between one
course and another one. And sometimes, it would appear, as a result of none.

And sometimes there is happiness here and sometimes there is not.
And sometimes all it takes to turn sadness into happiness is a thought
and at other times it takes more power and more energy than you think that
    you have got
and mistakes pile up in your chest as the night chills and suddenly you're
    caught

and you see that what happens happens for a reason if it happens at all
and reason implies a judgement and, tonight, that judgement is something small.

A Short Love Song

Because the winter is cold there is comfort in his arms
and in his bed and there's comfort in his soup
and in his eyes and in his home-baked midnight bread.

And as long as the winter lasts she'll drink his soup
and dunk his bread, crusty-edged and light as snow,
and when the spring comes back into their lives she'll go.

November Magus

It is early in the evening of a day halfway through November.
I am walking streets in the fog; lights halo, beam like smoke;
oranges and golds fill the street, rich and present.

A little later, standing outside my front door I look into the sky.
The moon is full and above the fog or mist and beyond the clouds
she is clear, vast and white and beautiful.

Below her I see Venus, the Evening Star, bright and bright and
slowly, ever so slowly, she moves towards me, shifting slightly
along my line of sight, a yellow point drifting in the sky,

and then it is clear I am watching a plane, and wing lights flash,
red and green and vanish into a bank of cloud.

                                        Goddess of Love,
cruising filled with lovers, hurtling out of my life into another country,

for a moment there you made me feel like a wise man.

Winter Lullaby

Sleep now my darling,
the winter is calling,
the daylight is dimming,
the snow will be falling.

Sleep now my darling,
be warm in the night,
sleep close to the stars,
use them for your light.

Sleep now my darling,
dream and breathe slow,
hold yourself close,
the winter will go.